Non-fiction Texts

Eileen Jones

Published in 2004 by:
Nelson Thornes Ltd
Delta Place
27 Bath Road
CHELTENHAM
GL53 7TH
United Kingdom

04 05 06 07 08 / 10 9 8 7 6 5 4 3 2 1

A catalogue record for this book is available from the British Library

ISBN 0-7487-8655-4

Illustrations by Martha Hardy, Brett Hudson (of GCI), Nick Schon and
Kate Sheppard.
Page make-up by GreenGate Publishing Services

Printed in Great Britain by Ashford Colour Press

Acknowledgements
All texts written by and copyright Eileen Jones except:

'Thor visits the land of the Giants' text copyright © Robert Nicholson. Reprinted
with permission of Two-Can Publishing, an imprint of Creative Publishing
International, Inc.; 'Plastic' text copyright © Two-Can Publishing, an imprint of
Creative Publishing International, Inc.; 'Connected Earth' screenshots copyright
© Connected Earth, BT 2004; 'Where you live', 'What else is in food' and 'Eating'
reproduced from *You and Your Body* by permission of Usborne Publishing, 83–85
Saffron Hill, London EC1N 8RT, UK copyright © 1993 Usborne Publishing Ltd;
'Jorvik' copyright © Jorvik 2004, Coppergate, YO1 9WT; 'Dictionary page' and
'Thesaurus' extracts reproduced from *The Usborne School Illustrated Dictionary
and Thesaurus* by permission of Usborne Publishing, 83–85 Saffron Hill, London
EC1N 8RT. Copyright © 2003 Usborne Publishing Ltd; BookBox screenshot
copyright © 4 Ventures Ltd 2003. Reproduced with permission from 4 Ventures
Ltd; 24 Hour Museum screenshots copyright © 24 Hour Museum
(www.show.me.uk).

Cover image: © NASA Our Sun from the Image of the Day Gallery

Contents

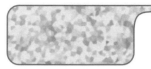

How to use this book

What this book contains

- Extracts from published works, plus tailor-made extracts, all arranged and chosen specifically to match the examples of medium-term planning provided by the National Literacy Strategy

- Teaching ideas for each extract to get you started, covering some of the relevant text, sentence or word level objectives from the relevant unit

How you can use *Classworks Literacy Texts* with other resources

- The blocked unit structure means you can dip into the book to find resources perfect for what you're teaching this week – it doesn't matter what plan, scheme or other resource you're using

- There are two *Classworks Literacy Texts* books for every year from Reception (or Primary 1) to Year 6 (or Primary 7): one contains Fiction and Poetry, the other contains Non-fiction. Both books together contain texts for every unit of the medium-term plans

What each page does

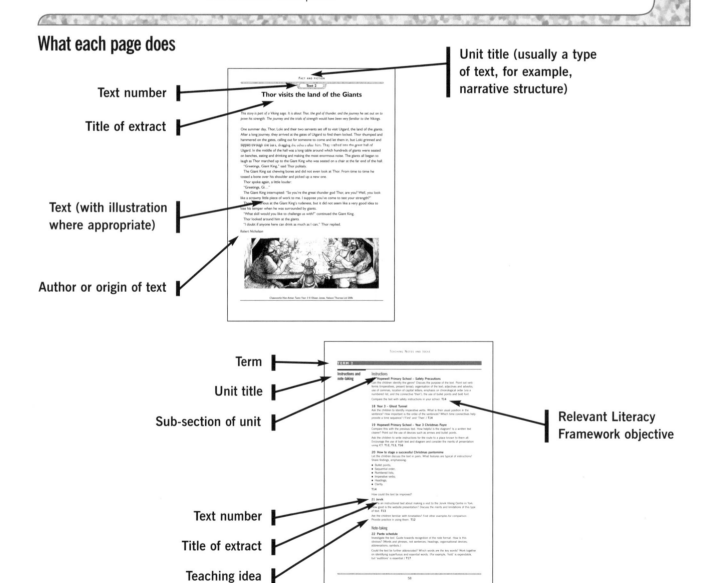

Text number

Title of extract

Text (with illustration where appropriate)

Author or origin of text

Unit title (usually a type of text, for example, narrative structure)

Term

Unit title

Sub-section of unit

Relevant Literacy Framework objective

Text number

Title of extract

Teaching idea

Text I

Viking Gods

The Vikings believed in many gods. The Viking people believed that different gods:

- controlled different parts of their lives;
- had different personalities; and
- did different jobs.

ODIN

Odin was the highest of the gods. He was the god of war, and the Vikings needed his protection in battle. He was admired for his wisdom and powers of magic.

THOR

Thor was the thunder god. He was worshipped for his strength and power. *Thursday* is named after him.

FREY

Frey made the crops grow. He kept the weather in balance. It was his job to make sure that there was enough sunshine and rain for a good harvest.

FREYA

Freya was the sister of Frey. She was the goddess of love and was famed for her beauty.

FRIGGA

Frigga was the family goddess. Her name is remembered in the word *Friday*

LOKI

Loki represented evil. Although he lived with the other gods in *Asgard*, their home, he often plotted to cause trouble among them.

Text 2

Thor visits the land of the Giants

This story is part of a Viking saga. It is about Thor, the god of thunder, and the journey he set out on to prove his strength. The journey and the trials of strength would have been very familiar to the Vikings.

One summer day, Thor, Loki and their two servants set off to visit Utgard, the land of the giants. After a long journey, they arrived at the gates of Utgard to find them locked. Thor thumped and hammered on the gates, calling out for someone to come and let them in, but Loki grinned and slipped through the bars, dragging the others after him. They walked into the great hall of Utgard. In the middle of the hall was a long table around which hundreds of giants were seated on benches, eating and drinking and making the most enormous noise. The giants all began to laugh as Thor marched up to the Giant King who was seated on a chair at the far end of the hall.

"Greetings, Giant King," said Thor politely.

The Giant King sat chewing bones and did not even look at Thor. From time to time he tossed a bone over his shoulder and picked up a new one.

Thor spoke again, a little louder:

"Greetings, Gi…"

The Giant King interrupted: "So you're the great thunder god Thor, are you? Well, you look like a scrawny little piece of work to me. I suppose you've come to test your strength?"

Thor was furious at the Giant King's rudeness, but it did not seem like a very good idea to lose his temper when he was surrounded by giants.

"What skill would you like to challenge us with?" continued the Giant King.

Thor looked around him at the giants.

"I doubt if anyone here can drink as much as I can," Thor replied.

Robert Nicholson

Famous Vikings

Vikings admired courage and daring. Many of their heroes were willing to make dangerous journeys.

Eric the Red

He was an explorer, journeying from Iceland to Greenland. In the year 986, he established a new colony there.

Leif Ericsson

He was the son of Eric the Red. He explored further afield, leading an expedition as far as North America. This was at the beginning of the 11th Century.

King Canute II

Between 1016 and 1028, Canute succeeded in gaining three thrones:

1. Denmark
2. England
3. Norway

He was known for his wisdom, and many stories were told about him.

Harald Haardraade

His fighting skills were famous. He was a member of the Varangian Guard, the most-feared unit in the armies of the 11th Century. In 1046, Harald Haardraade became King of Norway.

Classworks Non-fiction Texts Year 3 © Eileen Jones, Nelson Thornes Ltd 2004

Text 4

Melissa Rayford interviews...

History... with Alex Rhodes, modern historian

Why do you like History?

"History is just my favourite subject, and I have always liked it. I love producing interactive computer material set in different times."

What do you plan for the future?

"I want to become an archaeologist, so I need to study Ancient History. I plan to get another university qualification and then... who knows?"

What do you think of History on television?

"It makes me cross that some of the history television programmes are of a very poor standard. Why can't the producers make them all interesting and exciting? If people get bored, I think it is a waste of their licence money."

Do you have any advice to give?

"My only advice is to delve into your own past. You can find out the most amazing things."

Classworks Non-fiction Texts Year 3 © Eileen Jones, Nelson Thornes Ltd 2004

Text types

FOR SALE: a child's Budgie bicycle. Excellent condition – only 3 years old. Would suit a beginner. Stabilisers available if required.

Box no. 27

The **Bicycle** was invented in the 19th Century. Kirkpatrick Macmillan, a Scotsman, developed the use of pedals in 1840. The first real bicycle was produced in Paris in 1865. It soon acquired the nickname of *boneshaker*.

Once upon a time, there was a Princess who seemed to have everything.

"Tell me your instructions for the day," her maid requested every morning.

"Let me make you another fine outfit," begged the royal dressmaker each afternoon.

However, the Princess was not happy…

October 25
Nothing much happened at school. Mr Kerindi said he might be starting a football team, but he will only pick the best. I must practise my headers in garden for a while.

October 26
Can't believe it! I'm in the team. Practice is every Tuesday, so I'll miss Samsons, but I don't care!

Dick Whittington – The Village Playactors

Witheringham has had a rare treat: a stunning version of a favourite Christmas pantomime. All the cast are to be praised for their novel approach to the script and characters, but Carole Hewitt's name has to be the one in lights. She was the most comical **Cat** I have ever seen – quite stunning! Every word, gesture and facial expression had to be seen to be believed. Surely the West End beckons?

Metal

Metal is a material. It has many uses in the modern world.

Appearance and form

The appearance of this material is not always the same. It can vary in colour, weight and form, depending on how it is found. There are different types of metal. These types include:

- steel
- copper
- iron
- tin
- gold
- silver
- aluminium

How metals are found

Metals are not all found in the same way. A **nugget** of gold may be **mined** straight from deep within the ground. Other metals, such as iron, are found as **ores**, needing a heating or crushing process for their removal from their original rock state.

How we use metal

Examples of its use are everywhere. Metal is needed in our methods of transport. It is in electric cables, and is the material in cans for our food and drink.

Do we need metal?

Metal is now an essential part of everyday life. It seems impossible that we could manage without it.

Plastic

Plastic is a factory-made **material** that can be moulded into different shapes. It was first made in the USA about 90 years ago. Plastic is light but strong, and can be very colourful. It is useful because it doesn't fall apart easily, or **rust** in the open air. Often plastic is used to make things that used to be made from natural materials, such as wood or metal.

Plastic is stored as grains. The grains are melted down later on and poured into moulds.

How is plastic used?

Hard plastics are used to make chairs and crash helmets.

Plastic is used to strengthen other materials such as **fabric** for clothes.

Soft plastics are used to make shower curtains and dustbin bags.

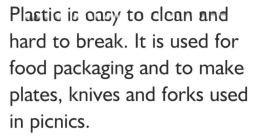

Plastic is easy to clean and hard to break. It is used for food packaging and to make plates, knives and forks used in picnics.

Plastic is not harmed by rain or snow, so it is used to make telephone booths.

Claire Llewellyn

Classworks Non-fiction Texts Year 3 © Eileen Jones, Nelson Thornes Ltd 2004

Text 8

Plastic (continued)

Plastic is made from oil, which is very valuable. The Earth's oil is being used up faster than fresh oil is being formed. One way of saving oil is to **recycle** plastic. Some places have recycling centres where different plastics are sorted. The plastics are taken to a factory where they are melted down and made into new things such as flower pots, traffic cones and dustbins.

Before recycling, plastic objects must be sorted into soft and hard plastics. Different kinds of plastics are recycled in different ways.

Did you know?

- The black lining inside a non-stick saucepan is a kind of plastic.

- Perspex is a strong, clear plastic. It is used to build see-through squash courts for squash matches, so that as many people as possible can watch.

- Plastic surgeons are named after the flexible or "plastic" skin that they mould.

Plastic in surgery

Some kinds of plastic are safe to use inside the human body. When people break their bones in an accident, the broken bones may be joined together again by plastic screws and pins.

Surgeons use different plastics for the thread that they use to sew up wounds, and to replace damaged parts of organs such as the heart.

Claire Llewellyn

Text 9

Connected Earth

How communication shapes the world

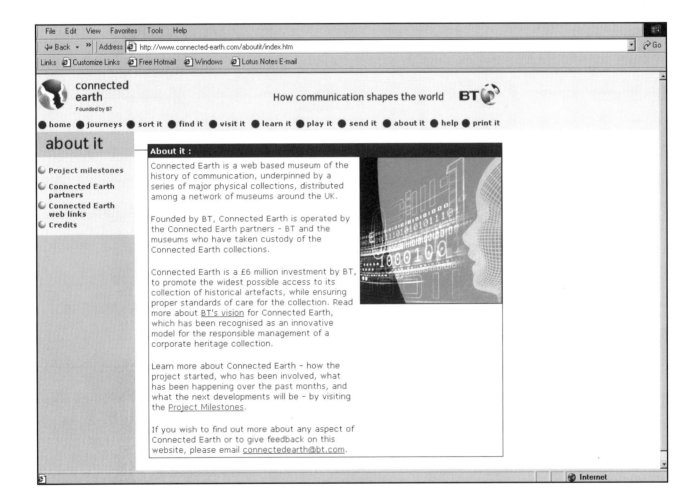

British Telecom

Text 10

Connected Earth (continued)

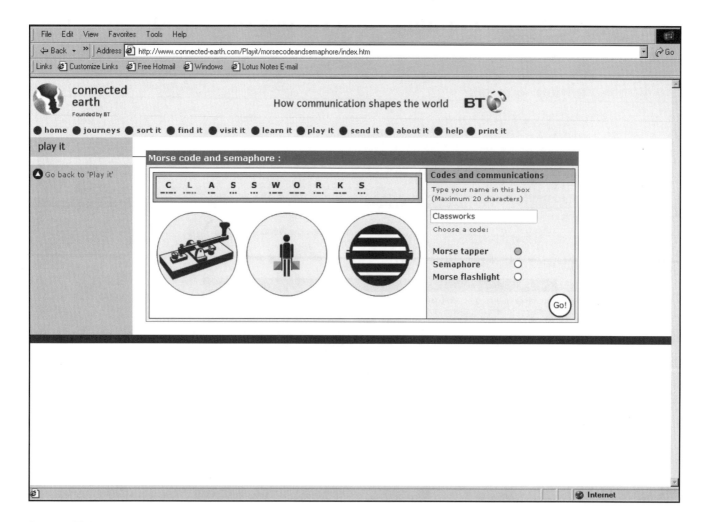

British Telecom

RSPCA

The RSPCA is a charitable organisation dedicated to the care of animals and well-known for its important work.

The reasons

In the first half of the nineteenth century, some animals were treated very badly. Cruel sports, such as cock-fighting, were still legal. In the fight against such cruelty, the RSPCA was established.

Size

The RSPCA has grown greatly since it began in 1824, and it does many types of work. There are currently over 300 uniformed RSPCA Inspectors and around 150 Animal Collection Officers working in England and Wales. Its first purpose is still the same: to abolish cruelty in the lives of animals.

The people

RSPCA Inspectors perform the work of the Society.

- they give advice;
- they investigate complaints;
- they check up on the welfare of animals causing concern;
- they find new homes for abandoned pets;
- they go into schools to give talks about animal care.

Do they need help?

The RSPCA always has too much work. Unpaid volunteers can do very useful work, such as distributing leaflets, or collecting money for the charity. The best way is to become an RSPCA **Member**.

The Members

RSPCA Members are people who join the Society. They help to spread word of the RSPCA's work. Anyone can apply to be a Member.

Where you live – Part 1

People's health is affected by where they live, what they do and how much money they have. Different illnesses are found in different parts of the world.

Weather

The weather can affect people's health. For instance, in hot, wet parts of the world, mosquitoes can spread a serious disease called malaria.

Mosquitoes can infect people with malaria when they bite them.

Food

In some poorer parts of the world, there is not always enough food to go around. Without all the goodness they need from food, people can get very ill. This is called malnutrition.

Shaded areas on this map show poorer parts of the world.

In parts of Africa, many people die every year from malnutrition.

Not all food is good for you. In richer parts of the world many people suffer from diseases which doctors think may be caused by eating too much of the wrong kind of food.

Susan Meredith, Kate Needham, Mike Unwin

This meal has lots of sugar and fat, which is bad for you.

Where you live – Part 2

Pollution

Pollution can harm all living things, including people. For instance, polluted lakes and rivers can make people ill if the water gets into their drinking supplies.

Overcrowding

Illness can spread quickly in places where people live crowded together without good health care. A disease that infects many people at one time in this way is called an epidemic.

In 1990 an epidemic of cholera in South America affected many people who lived in poor places like the one in this picture.

Jobs

The places where people work, and the jobs they do, can affect their health.

Knowing the facts

Learning about how your body works and how illnesses happen helps you live a healthier life.

Years ago nobody knew that smoking caused serious heart and lung diseases. Now people can learn to stay healthier by not smoking.

People who work down mines can suffer breathing problems from the dust.

Susan Meredith, Kate Needham, Mike Unwin

Text 14

What else is in food?

The food you eat also has tiny amounts of nutrients called vitamins and minerals which you need.

What do vitamins do?

Vitamins are like little workers which help other nutrients to do their jobs. There are about 20 different kinds. Most are named after the letters of the alphabet.

The chart below shows what some vitamins do and where you find them.

A

Vitamin A helps you see in the dark. You find it in egg yolks, liver, full fat milk and carrots.

B

There are lots of kinds of B vitamins, each with a different job. Cereals, dairy products and meat have B vitamins.

C

Vitamin C is good for health and body repairs. You find it in fresh fruit and vegetables.

D

Vitamin D helps make your bones and teeth strong. You get it from eggs, fish and butter.

Sailors used to get scurvy – a disease which stops wounds from healing. This is because they were at sea for months without any fresh vegetables or fruit and so no vitamin C.

Your body can make vitamin D itself using sunlight. People who live in less sunny countries need extra vitamin D from their food.

Susan Meredith, Kate Needham, Mike Unwin

Eating

Your body needs food and drink to keep working properly.

Using your teeth

You use your teeth to make your food small enough to swallow. Your front teeth are a different shape from your back teeth. Can you feel the difference with your tongue?

The outside of your teeth is the hardest part of you. It is made of strong stuff called enamel.

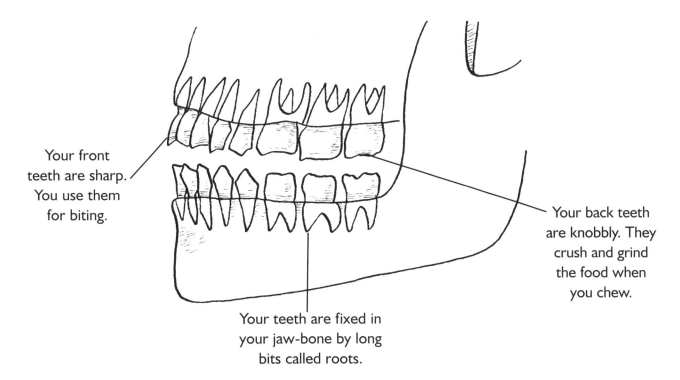

Your front teeth are sharp. You use them for biting.

Your back teeth are knobbly. They crush and grind the food when you chew.

Your teeth are fixed in your jaw-bone by long bits called roots.

Two sets of teeth

Your first set of teeth are called milk teeth because they grow when you are a baby. There are 20 of these.

There are 32 teeth in a full adult set. Nobody really knows why people grow two sets of teeth.

Susan Meredith, Kate Needham, Mike Unwin

Classworks Non-fiction Texts Year 3 © Eileen Jones, Nelson Thornes Ltd 2004

Eating (continued)

Food

Different foods do different jobs in your body. You need to eat small amounts of lots of different kinds of food to stay really healthy.

Potatoes, rice, pasta, bread and sweet food give you energy.

Milk, cheese and yogurt make your bones and teeth strong.

Foods such as meat, fish and eggs make you grow and help to repair your body.

Fruit and vegetables have vitamins in them. These keep your body working efficiently.

Cleaning teeth

It is important to clean your teeth well, especially last thing at night.

Tiny bits of food and drink stick to your teeth even though you cannot feel them.

If bits are left on your teeth, chemicals called acids are made. The acids make holes in your teeth.

Susan Meredith, Kate Needham, Mike Unwin

Classworks Non-fiction Texts Year 3 © Eileen Jones, Nelson Thornes Ltd 2004

Hopewell Primary School

SAFETY PRECAUTIONS

Take time to read these:

1. If an alarm sounds, **OBEY** it.

2. Proceed immediately to the closest illuminated EXIT sign.

3. Walk quickly, but calmly.

4. Get out of the building.

5. Then assemble on the surrounding lawn.

6. Listen to the appointed wardens for further instructions.

● Do **NOT** run.

● Do **NOT** stop to collect personal possessions.

● Do **NOT** panic.

Year 3 – Ghost Tunnel

How to find us

1   First come into the school through the main door.
2   Then turn left into the hall.
3   Dodge the people selling raffle tickets.
4   Rush straight past the *Ticket Tombola*.
5   Turn right at *Guess the Dog's Weight*.
6   Ignore two stalls selling clothes.
7   Watch out for a banner saying **YEAR 3**.
8   Make your way to the ***Entrance*** sign.
9   Get ready to be scared!
10 Finally tunnel your way in.

Classworks Non-fiction Texts Year 3 © Eileen Jones, Nelson Thornes Ltd 2004

Hopewell Primary School

Year 3 Christmas Fayre

Takes place on Friday, December 1st.

Doors open at 6 o'clock. **Be early.**

Watch out for the

GHOST TUNNEL

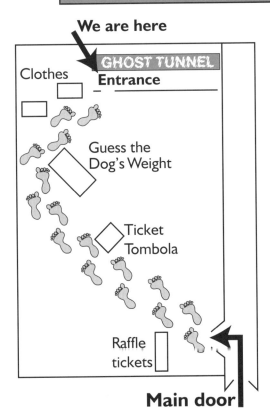

We are here

GHOST TUNNEL

Clothes

Entrance

Guess the
Dog's Weight

Ticket
Tombola

Raffle
tickets

Main door

Don't miss the
Year 3 experience.

Text 20

How to stage a successful Christmas pantomime

What you need:

- a suitable hall and stage
- a good play script (a well-known story, or your own version)
- a supply of costumes
- simple props
- lighting (if available)
- four weeks to prepare

How to organise yourselves:

1 Begin work four weeks before the performance.
2 Choose a producer.
3 Make photocopies of the script.
4 Hold auditions, reading parts of the script.
5 Allocate parts, with the producer's decision always being final.
6 Start rehearsals.
7 Make lists of essential costumes and props and arrange for them to be made.
8 Continue with rehearsals.
9 Collect props and costumes.
10 Paint scenery as required.
11 Create and display advertising posters.
12 Check seating, parking and safety arrangements.
13 Print and distribute tickets.
14 Try out the lighting.
15 Make sure everyone knows their lines.
16 Hold a final dress rehearsal.
17 Have a great show!

Classworks Non-fiction Texts Year 3 © Eileen Jones, Nelson Thornes Ltd 2004

Text 21

Jorvik

Jorvik

Text 22

Panto schedule

Script

1. *4 Oct*: Set groups to write scenes of *Jack and the Giant Sunflower*→
2. *25 Oct*: put together/change bits→
3. *1 Nov*: complete script→

People

1. *4 Nov*: hold auditions
2. Trial readings
3. *11 Nov*: final casting

Putting together

- Rehearsals – 2/3 times a week
- Order lights
- Ask parents for costumes & props
- Spare children (& Bob?) paint scenery
- Secretary – letters, tickets, safety regs
- Caretaker – chairs, parking

Final countdown

- Dress rehearsal (with lights) – *30 Nov*
- **Show: 1, 2, 3 Dec**

Classworks Non-fiction Texts Year 3 © Eileen Jones, Nelson Thornes Ltd 2004

Text 23

Flow chart of pantomime schedule

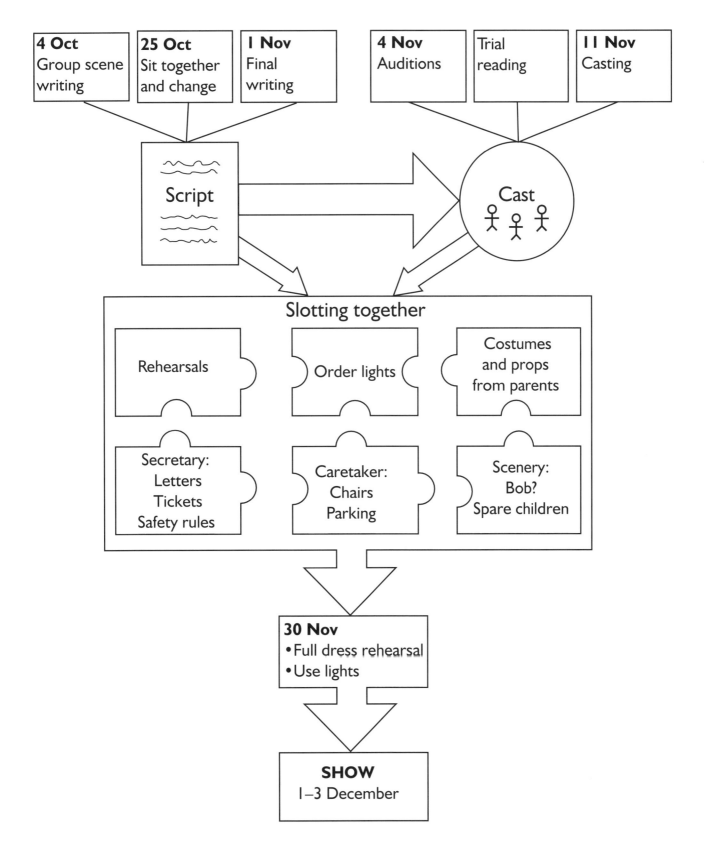

Text 24

Week off school!

Trip — Isle of Wight

Only us and Yr 4

Cost = £60

Whole week off school! May 15 — 19

Good places to go to

Trips & sporty things

4 teachers & some parents

* MUST HAVE QUICK ANSWER

TONIGHT'S JOBS:

•persuade Mum

•get letter signed

•give back to Mr Wilkins by Fri

• £5 deposit by week on Mon

Text 25

Educational visit notes

Equipment: overhead projector, slides of Isle of Wight, spare letters

1. Location

- Isle of Wight (* <u>show slides</u>)
- LEA premises
- Good, safe facilities

2. Staff

- 4 teachers + 6 trained helpers + first aider
- All trained minibus drivers
- Considerable school trip experience

3. Timetable

- Daily sports: swimming/orienteering/tennis/indoor gym
- Trips:

    Local beaches

    Wildlife centre

    Pottery

    Museums

4. Practical details

Cost: £60

Deposit – £5, payable by Mon 10th Jan

Signed permission needed

Warm, practical clothes

PE kit; swimwear; strong walking shoes

Info to me on medical matters

5. Final words

- Great opportunity
- Good for self-confidence

If money a problem, please speak to me

Classworks Non-fiction Texts Year 3 © Eileen Jones, Nelson Thornes Ltd 2004

Dictionary page

decrepit d

deception (n) a trick that makes people believe something that is not true. **deceptive** (adj). **deceptively** (adv).

decibel (n) unit for measuring the volume of sound.

decide *deciding decided*
1 (v) to make up your mind about something.
2 (v) to settle something. *The vote was decided by a show of hands.*

deciduous (adj) Trees that are **deciduous** shed their leaves every year.

decimal
1 (adj) A **decimal** system uses units of tens, hundreds, thousands, etc. *Decimal currency.*
2 **decimal point** (n) a dot separating whole numbers from tenths, hundredths, thousandths, etc. *The numbers 2.5, 3.75, and 4.624 all use decimal points.*
3 (n) a fraction, or a whole number and a fraction, written with a decimal point. *0.5, 6.37, and 82.54 are all decimals.*

decipher *deciphering deciphered*
(v) to work out something that is written in code or is hard to understand. *I can't decipher Jim's handwriting.* **decipherable** (adj).

decision (n) If you make a **decision**, you make up your mind about something.

decisive (adj) If you are **decisive**, you make choices quickly and easily. **decisively** (adv).

deck
1 (n) the floor of a boat or ship. See **ship**
2 (n) (US) a platform with railings on the outside of a building, usually high up (balcony, UK).

declare *declaring declared*
1 (v) to say something firmly. *Justin declared that he would never eat meat again.* **declaration** (n).
2 (v) to announce something formally. *The government declared that the war was over.* **declaration** (n).
3 (v) When you **declare** in a cricket match, you end your team's innings.

decline *declining declined*
1 (v) to turn something down, or to refuse something. *I'm afraid we must decline your invitation.*
2 (v) to get worse, or to get smaller. *Ludwig's health began to decline. The population of our village is declining.* **decline** (n).

decode *decoding decoded* (v) to turn something that is written in code into ordinary language.

decompose *decomposing decomposed* (v) to rot, or to decay. **decomposition** (n).

decongestant (n) a drug that unblocks your nose, chest, etc. when you have a cold. **decongestion** (n).

decontaminate *decontaminating decontaminated* (v) to remove radioactive or other harmful substances from something or some place. **decontamination** (n).

decorate *decorating decorated*
1 (v) If you **decorate** something, you add things to it to make it prettier. **decoration** (n), **decorative** (adj).
2 (v) If you decorate a room or house, you paint it or put up wallpaper. **decoration** (n) **decorator** (n).

decrease *decreasing decreased*
1 (v) to become less, smaller or fewer. *I have noticed a marked decrease in enthusiasm for this project.* **decreasing** (adj), **decreasingly** (adv).
2 (n) a loss, or the amount by which something lessens.

decree *decreeing decreed* (v) to give an order that must be obeyed. *The teacher decreed that there should be no more cheating.* **decree** (n).

decrepit (adj) old and feeble.

Jane Bingham, Fiona Chandler

Classworks Non-fiction Texts Year 3 © Eileen Jones, Nelson Thornes Ltd 2004

Text 27

Thesaurus

willing

wedding see **marriage 2.**

weird see **stranger 1, 2.**

welcome
(adj) Emily's parents made me feel welcome. at home, one of the family, accepted, appreciated, wanted, included.
OPPOSITES: unwelcome, excluded.

well
1 (adj) you look well. healthy, fit, in good health, blooming, strong, robust, thriving.
OPPOSITES: unwell, ill.
2 (n) The well provided water for the village. water hole, borehole, spring, water source, oasis, artesian well, wishing well.

well-behaved
(adj) A well-behaved child. good, obedient, cooperative, amenable, compliant, docile, polite, well-mannered, dutiful.
OPPOSITES: badly behaved, naughty.

well-known see **famous**

wet
1 (adj) My clothes are wet. damp, soaking, dripping, sopping wet, sodden, drenched, wringing wet, saturated, wet, through.
OPPOSITES: dry, bone-dry (informal).
2 (adj) After the rain, the ground was wet. damp, moist, sodden, spongy, muddy, dewy.
OPPOSITES: dry, parched.
3 (adj) If it's wet we won't go out. rainy, raining, pouring, drizzly, showery, damp, misty, dank, clammy, humid.
OPPOSITES: dry, fine.

4 (adj) (informal) Stand up for yourself and don't be so wet! See **weak 3.**
5 (v) Wet the cloth. dampen, moisten, soak, drench, saturate, steep, douse, splash, sprinkle, spray, irrigate (ground).

whine
1 (v) The toddler began to whine. whimper, wail, grizzle, cry (informal).
2 (v) Cecil always finds something to whine about. See **complain.**

whip see **beat 1, 4.**

whirl
(v) Watch the dancers whirl round the room. spin, twirl, swirl, circle, wheel, reel, pirouette, gyrate, revolve, swivel.

whisper
1 (v) I can't hear you when you whisper. speak under your breath, speak in hushed tones, talk quietly, speak softly, keep your voice down, murmur, mutter.
2 (n) Sandy spoke in a whisper. low voice, quiet voice, soft voice, murmur, stage whisper, undertone, hushed tones (plural).

white
1 (adj) The statue looked white in the moonlight. milky, chalky, pearly, silvery, snow-white, alabaster, ivory, ghostly.
2 (adj) Granny has white hair. snowy, snow-white, silver, hoary.
3 (adj) Edmund's face was white with fear. ashen, pale, pallid, bloodless, wan, pasty, waxen, chalky, drained.

whole
(adj) Will the whole film be shown on television? entire,

complete, full, total, uncut, unedited, unabridged (book).

wicked
1 (adj) A wicked criminal. evil, bad, sinful, immoral, corrupt, depraved, villainous, vicious, vile, fiendish, diabolical, devilish, black-hearted, lawless.
OPPOSITES: good, virtuous.
2 (adj) A wicked grin. See **mischievous 2.**

wide see **broad 1, 2.**

wild
1 (adj) That dog is quite wild. untamed, undomesticated, savage, fierce, ferocious.
OPPOSITES: tame, domesticated.
2 (adj) We crossed some wild country. uncultivated, unspoilt, untamed, natural, deserted, empty, waste, barren, desolate, bleak, rough, rugged, overgrown.
OPPOSITES: cultivated, inhabited.
3 (adj) What wild weather! See **stormy 1.**
4 (adj) The boys are wild. rowdy, boisterous, unruly, uncontrollable, undisciplined, wayward, out of control, rough, noisy, violent, rude, riotous.
5 (adj) Ziggy had a wild idea. See **mad 3.**
6 (adj) Al is wild about soccer. See **mad 5.**

willing
(adj) Helen is always willing to help. glad, happy, pleased, ready, quick, prepared, eager, keen, game (informal).

Jane Bingham, Fiona Chandler

Text 28

Notes in class

Joe! What did you eat for lunch? I think Brain has really poisoned me this time! I've felt sick ever since I had her rotten chicken nuggets.

Coming to football practice?

Ben

Careful! Nearly got caught then. I won't be going anywhere if I get caught again. Same here - I felt really funny, even though I had a hamburger. Wish my Mum would let me bring a packed lunch.

Joe

Meet in cloakroom before football?

Ben

Text 29

Claire

2pm

Claire,
So sorry to disturb you, in the middle of a lesson,
but I have a problem.

I am feeling quite strange. Everything seems
to be spinning, and I feel increasingly sick.
I have tried sitting with my head between
my knees, but I think that I've only succeeded
in making myself worse. It certainly doesn't help
that the children keep pestering me, asking me
what I'm doing.

You know I'm not one to make a fuss — but
the fact is I'm on playground duty this afternoon,
and I really don't feel well enough to go out.
Would you mind doing my duty?

I know it's a lot to ask, but I'll do your
duty on Friday.

Thanks a million!

Andrew

Andrew

2.20 pm

Andrew

I am sorry to let you down. Normally I would not hesitate to change duties, but I have already made arrangements to go home. An unbearable migraine, dizziness and nausea since about one o'clock have made Junior 5 even more insufferable than usual.

The Head is coming to take my class, so I'm afraid there is no hope of her helping you out. Have you tried Mina?
Really sorry,

Claire

URGENT!

THIS SCHOOL IS CLOSED ENTRY IS STRICTLY PROHIBITED

Unforeseen circumstances necessitate that Hopewell School is closed until further notice.

Children must not return until a formal announcement is made.

Announcements will be made via local radio and television stations, and through the Press.

SIGNED *Alfred Pickle*

County Education Officer

Text 32

HOPELESS HOPEWELL!

Why is Hopewell closed?

By Sharina Kaar

This week brought more problems to the already troubled Hopewell School. Yesterday morning, doors and gates were locked, with a notice signed by the Local Education Officer barring entry. No information was given about a re-opening date.

The cause of the closure remains unknown, but rumours abound. There has been talk of a staff walk-out, insect infestation and unruly and uncontrollable pupils. However, confirmation of any of the theories is difficult to secure.

"I know for a fact that three teachers went home sick during Wednesday afternoon," said Gaynor Watkins, a 33-year-old parent.

Other parents spoke of their children being ill on Wednesday afternoon; and one girl in Junior 5 saw her teacher looking very pale.

"She was just sitting there, holding her head and moaning," reported 10-year-old Becky Wright. "She didn't even bother teaching us anything."

Why was there illness on Wednesday afternoon? Doubts have been raised before about the skills of Hopewell's cook. Mrs Brain may have gone too far this time.

Text 33

Dear Mr Pickle

"The Cabin"
Flaxen Way,
Asperton,
WL6 8FY

14th February 2004

Mr A Pickle
County Education Officer
Larkshire Education Authority
22 Eastgate Street
Asperton
WL6 4VS

Dear Mr Pickle,

Can you please explain what is happening? My daughter, a high achiever, has now been without a school to attend for four days. This is totally unacceptable!

As a tax-paying member of the community, I have a right to free education for my children. Therefore, alternative teaching arrangements should have been put into place immediately. As a parent and a PTA committee member, I am appalled at the failure of the Education Authority to make such provision.

Unless this matter is settled quickly, and my Becky, very distressed by this disruption, begins to receive her rightful education, I shall be seeking legal advice.

Yours sincerely,

Annabelle Wright

Annabelle Wright

Text 34

Dear Jane

"The Cabin"
Flaxen Way,
Asperton,
WL6 8FY

14th February

Dear Jane,

I am so fed up with Hopewell! You just won't believe what the latest thing is: closed until further notice!

There was a problem last Wednesday afternoon. Becky told me that some of her class felt ill. As well as that, her teacher was doing even less work than usual – just sitting holding her head, moaning.

The next morning, I intended finding out why Becky had been left sitting doing no work for an hour (you know how quick she is). What did we find? The school was locked up. Quite honestly, I'm thinking of moving Becky to a place where the teachers make a little more effort, and standards are higher. Hopewell just seems to lurch from one disaster to another.

We'll talk about it next weekend – looking forward to seeing you,

Fond regards,

Annabelle

Annabelle

Text 35

Dear Mrs Wright

At Least We Try

Larkshire Education Authority

22 Eastgate Street, Asperton, WL6 4VS

"The Cabin"
Flaxen Way
Asperton
WL6 8FY

19th February 2004

Dear Mrs Wright

I was sorry to read of Becky's distress, and your own understandable concerns.

My decision to close Hopewell was not taken lightly. At this very moment, all staff here are working full-time, putting in place final arrangements for the school to re-open. Nevertheless, I would not wish Becky, or indeed her fellow school pupils, to return to anything other than perfection. With your PTA experience you will, I am sure, understand this need for caution.

Yours sincerely

Alfred Pickle

Alfred Pickle
County Education Officer

Text 36

The Case of the School Meal Poisoner

Mrs Kalides has asked her class to write a story. She thinks the new girl's story is particularly imaginative… or is it?

The Case of the School Meal Poisoner

The School Cook was Mrs Brain. She was awful! If it was possible to make food look strange, taste unpleasant or smell peculiar, she managed to do it. In all the time I was at that school, I did not enjoy a single meal. Nevertheless, even I did not guess at what was to come.

It all started one afternoon in February. During the first lesson, some of us started to feel ill. Tracey sat with her head in her hands; Matt was clutching his stomach, groaning; and Jade had to lie on the floor. I had a sort of ringing in my ears, and I felt really dizzy.

Some of us asked Miss Bone to ring our parents, but she acted as if she could not hear properly. She was either busy writing and reading notes, or just sitting staring into space, holding her head and moaning.

Well, that evening my mother started an investigation. She got on the phone to all her friends and made a list of all the children who had gone home ill – plus any teachers she knew about. She thought that there were just too many coincidences. She decided…

Classworks Non-fiction Texts Year 3 © Eileen Jones, Nelson Thornes Ltd 2004

Health and safety

Local Authorities have strict rules about the preparation of food. Kitchens and all equipment should be kept scrupulously clean. Workers are required to wear uniforms. Gloves must be worn when food is handled, and hair covered and tied back.

These rules are strict, but they need to be. Each year, thousands of cases of food poisoning are reported to County Medical Officers. In addition, many less serious cases are probably left unreported. The health problem remains a serious one.

In the case of a fit, healthy adult, food poisoning usually presents little danger. However, for the elderly and the very young, the dangers are greater. Old people, babies and young children have weaker powers of resistance, with their **immune systems** less able to cope with the effects of an attack. **Dehydration** can occur quickly, and hospital treatment may be necessary.

It is essential, therefore, that if suspicions are held about the standards of hygiene in a school kitchen, the Local Authority is alerted. Immediately, the kitchen staff will be stopped from preparing and serving food, and the school will be closed while thorough checks are made. Greater vigilance is the only way to improve the country's health and safety.

Text 38

Health and safety – note-taking

KEY POINTS

- **Local Authority rules for food** = v. strict

- **Kitchens** – v. clean

- **Workers**:
  - uniforms
  - food gloves
  - hair back & covered

- **food poisoning** ev. yr. 000s (reported to County Medical Officer – some more not reported)

- **dangers** – food p.
  - OK: if fit adult
  - Bad: babies, children & old people
  - Can get DEHYDRATED – need hospital

- **Action**
  - Tell LA so school closed
  - More CARE – so health & safety better

Dear Year 3

Get Wise
Heathfield High School

25th November

Dear Year 3

We are staging our own production of Roald Dahl's *Fantastic Mr Fox*. We know that you have made a study of this book, and we are sure you would enjoy our version of this wonderful tale.

Our dress rehearsal is on Thursday, 6th December at 2.00pm. Please let us know if you are able to attend this.

We look forward to having you as an audience.

Best wishes,

Stacey Blair

Stacey Blair
Year 7 Prefect

Text 40

Dear Stacey

Always First
Allsgood Junior and Infant School

28th November

Dear Stacey,

Thank you very much for your invitation. It was very thoughtful of you to invite us.

We were all very pleased to read your letter. *Fantastic Mr Fox* is one of our favourite stories, so we are longing to see your play.

We hope the rehearsals are going well. We will see you on Thursday 6th December.

Best wishes,

Year 3

Shelley   Sarah   Nishpa   Duane

Simon   Tom   Harry   Meera

Carl   Laura   Ben   Ramid   Max

Don   Daisy   Matt   Chris   Emma

Charley

Classworks Non-fiction Texts Year 3 © Eileen Jones, Nelson Thornes Ltd 2004

Citizenship

agreeing with others 2
anger 5
arguments 3, 4

beliefs 38
bullying 22–23

change 18, 22, 25
Christianity 41–42
concern for:
    – animals 17
    – other people 11

danger 25
death 25
divorce 22

emotions 5, 11, 14, 17, 18, 22
environmental issues 55–65

families 20–22
fear 14,
feelings 5, 11, 14, 17, 18, 22
festivals 38–42
friendships 1, 3

gods 38–42
growing up 18

happiness 1, 20
Hinduism 42
home 20–21

Glossary

ally	friend; one who helps
amity	friendship
community	people living near one another; working together
conservation	saving and caring for the environment
consideration	thought for others
culture	a set of beliefs and traditions
enmity	the state of being enemies
faith	a religious belief
fellowship	helping one another
global	belonging to the world
humanity	kindness and fairness
kin	family
malice	ill-feeling
maturity	the state of being grown-up
multicultural	from many cultures
nation	country
national	belonging to one nation
nationality	the country of birth
peril	danger
poverty	having little or no money
reconciliation	becoming friends again
refugee	person who needs to leave his home country
respect	treating others with consideration and avoiding insulting behaviour
tolerance	acceptance of others and other attitudes

A–Z Lower Markham

ABBREVIATIONS

Av.	Avenue
Cl.	Close
Cres.	Crescent
Dr.	Drive
E.	East
Gdn.	Garden
Gdns.	Gardens
Nth.	North
Pk.	Park
Pl.	Place
Rd.	Road
Squ.	Square
St.	Street
Sth.	South
Ter.	Terrace
W.	West
Wk.	Walk
Yd.	Yard

Text 44

A–Z Lower Markham (continued)

A

Abbey Cl. MK8 .... 3F **25**
Abbey Rd. MK8 .... 3F **25**
Abbotsfield Way MK8 .... 3E **25**
Abergavenny Dr. MK9 .... 2B **18**
Adams Rd. MK3 .... 2B **19**
Admiral Cres. MK16 .... 5C **15**
Agnes Dr. MK16 .... 3E **15**
Albion Rd. MK3 .... 2B **19**
Albion Wk. MK3 .... 2B **19**
Almay St. MK16 .... IE **15**
Ashdown Dr. MK4 .... 2A **21**
Avis St. Nth. MK8 .... 3F **25**
Avis St. Sth. MK8 .... 3G **25**

B

Banbury Av. MK16 .... 5E **15**
Banbury Rd. MK16 .... 5E **15**
Barking Hill MK4 .... IC **21**
Bedworth St. MK11 .... 6F **14**
Bibstone Way MK2 .... 2B **13**
Brixham Cres. MK4 .... IC **8**
Brixham Dr. MK4 .... ID **8**
Brixham Rd. MK4 .... 2D **8**

Text 45

Website – BookBox

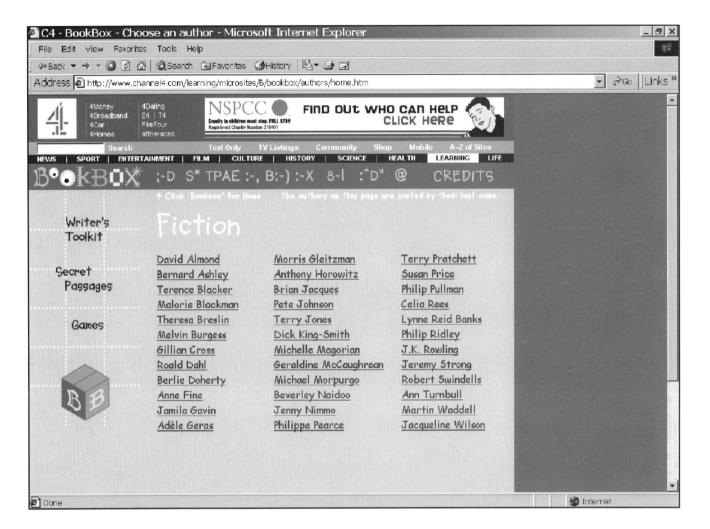

4 Ventures Ltd

Text 46

Website – 24 Hour Museum Trail for Harry Potter Fans

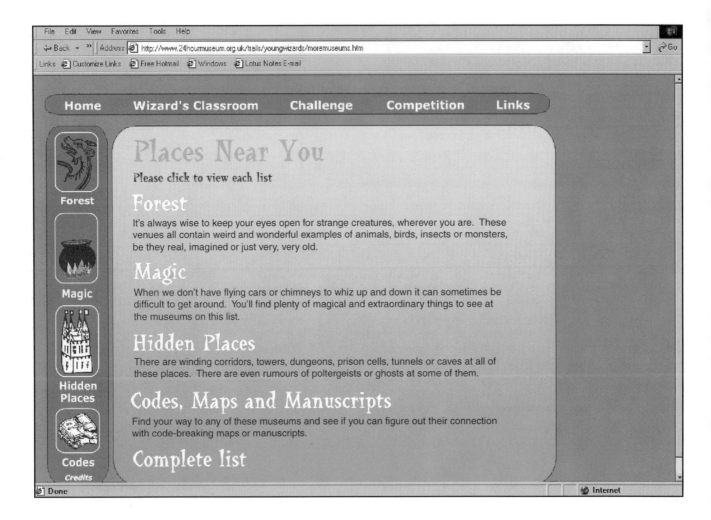

24 Hour Museum (www.show.me.uk)

Text 47

Website – 24 Hour Museum Trail for Harry Potter Fans (continued)

24 Hour Museum (www.show.me.uk)

Contents

Classworks Non-fiction Texts Year 3 © Eileen Jones, Nelson Thornes Ltd 2004

Index

Guide to Hopewell Primary School

ASSEMBLY

Assembly is held daily, with Infants and Juniors catered for separately. Friday's assembly is always a whole school celebration, and parents are invited to attend.

CLASSROOMS

All our classrooms are spacious, well-lit and airy. Seating is arranged in groups, with tables accommodating four to six children. A calm but busy working atmosphere is fostered.

LIBRARY

The library is situated next to the Dining Hall. Recently refurbished, it is an attractive, well-planned room. A qualified librarian is employed, and all the children are trained to use the Dewey system.

LUNCH

Nourishing, cooked lunches are prepared on the premises. Fresh ingredients are used, and Mrs Brain and her team produce imaginative, unusual meals. If preferred, the children may choose to bring a packed lunch.

PLAYTIME

The school regards playtimes as important parts of the day. Teachers and trained supervisors ensure a safe, inclusive, happy atmosphere.

Classworks Non-fiction Texts Year 3 © Eileen Jones, Nelson Thornes Ltd 2004

Teaching notes and ideas

Fact and fiction

1 Viking Gods

Talk about content and likely context. Point out that the text deals with **facts** about the Viking beliefs. Would you find it in the **fiction** or **non-fiction** section of the library? (Non-fiction.)

Investigate style and structure, asking the children to identify aspects unlikely to be met in a fictional text (bullet points; headings; organisational and presentational devices; a focus on clear statement and presentation).

Discuss other ways to present this information (more headings; sub-headings; different layout). Model some examples. **T17, T18, S9**

2 Thor visits the land of the Giants

Is this fiction or non-fiction? (Fiction.) Investigate the differences in style from the last text:

- a traditional, story-telling opening (One summer day, ...);
- greater use of description and detail (adjectives, adverbs and expressive verbs);
- absence of headings or helpful organisational devices;
- less formal tone and style.

Work together, identifying instances of the above. **T17**

Revise the term 'verb', and consider its needs and function. Give practice in collecting examples of verbs. Can you put any of them into groups? (For example: 'said', 'interrupted', 'replied'.) Ask the children to make their own additions to the groups. **S3, S5**

3 Famous Vikings

Focus on presentation. Ask the children for their comments. Prompt awareness of headings; different font sizes; organisational devices.

Explore other factual texts on your current history topic. Collect examples of a range of presentational devices. **S9**

4 Melissa Rayford interviews...

Explain that non-fiction texts can take a variety of forms. This is a text dealing largely with personal opinion. Discuss the possible context (a newspaper or magazine article). Ask the children to identify devices used for presentation. Explore their purposes. **S9**

5 Text types

Revise your definitions of:

- fact;
- fiction;
- non-fiction.

Set the task of applying one of the labels to each of these texts. Ask the children to be ready to justify their choices. Share results, encouraging discussion. Are there any texts that present problems? **T17**

Speaking and listening

Discuss what the children have learned about types of fiction and non-fiction writing.

Make sure that they are confident in their use of the terms 'fact', 'fiction' and 'non-fiction'.

Reports

6 Metal

Identify the text as a **report**. Explain that a report describes the way things are. Identify some important features:

- an opening statement;
- use of paragraphs;
- non-chronological order;
- appropriate, impersonal style;
- correct names and words;
- helpful layout;
- headings.

Compile a class list of report features. **T18**

What are the main points in this text? Help the children to identify key words and phrases. **T20**

7 Plastic

Point out the clarity of this text. How is this achieved? Why are some words in bold print? (Later defined in a glossary?) Ask the children to make notes, identifying the main four or five points and key words and phrases. **T20**

8 Plastic (continued)

Could the layout be improved? Share ideas, considering the use of further presentational devices, such as sub-headings. **S9**

Ask the children to make notes, again identifying the main points and key words and phrases. Combine these with notes from Text 7. How will you present the information? **T21, T22**

9–10 Connected Earth

Discuss modern ICT-based sources for information, such as this text. Consider differences in layout; the visual element; a mixture of instructions and reports.

Do internet research for a report on your current work in another subject. Is it quicker than using a book? What are the advantages and disadvantages? **T19, T20**

11 RSPCA

Ask the children to consider how they could add to this report (supplying facts and figures; providing information about applying for a leaflet; how to request a school visit). Let the children do research for the additional information. Stress the need to think also about how to present the information. **T19, T20**

12 Where you live – Part 1

Compare the report's layout with those of previous texts. Is information easy to access? Where could more headings and sub-headings be helpful? **T19**

Use the text for word and spelling work. Focus on a letter combination (for example 'ea': spread; health; eating; areas; year; diseases; meal) or common spelling difficulties (different; every; serious). Identify new words. Look for ways to group words, and add them to spelling logs and personal dictionaries. **W6, W13**

13 Where you live – Part 2
Point out the change in font size for some parts (for example, 'In 1990…'). Why is this done? Responses should include answers such as: these are facts, additional to the main report; a different font size makes the words noticeable. Provide practice in using headings and sub-headings by asking the children to set questions for a partner. How quickly and easily can information be located? **T18**

Ask the children to identify the four or five key points covered. Can they identify key words and phrases? **T20**

Use the two texts to compile a simple record sheet, charting key links between ill-health and the environment. Focus on the use of key words. **T21**

14 What else is in food?
Discuss layout variety. Is the chart helpful? Is information clear? How would you have written the text? Ask the children to write the section on vitamins with paragraphs, headings, and supplying additional information. **T19**

Investigate the use of commas to separate items in a list. Ask the children to identify examples. Use them as models for the children's own writing. **S13**

15–16 Eating
Ask the children to refer to the original list of report features. Which of those features are evident in this text?

Focus on layout and presentation. Set questions on the subject matter. Do the children know where in the text to search for the answer? Which devices prove helpful? **S9**

Look again at the chart in Text 14. Set the task of creating an information chart, (perhaps working in pairs), extracting key points from this text, as well as other science texts. Stress the need for clear presentation. **T21**

Speaking and listening
Discuss reports in your classroom (for example, a report on the results of the Christmas Fayre/Red Nose Day collection/latest meeting of the PTA). Talk about the different ways of presenting information.

Let individuals share examples of their own work.

TERM 2

Instructions and note-taking

Instructions

17 Hopewell Primary School – Safety Precautions

Can the children identify the genre? Discuss the purpose of the text. Point out verb forms (imperatives, present tense); organisation of the text; adjectives and adverbs; use of commas; location of capital letters; emphasis on chronological order (via a numbered list, and the connective 'then'); the use of bullet points and bold font.

Compare the text with safety instructions in your school. **T14**

18 Year 3 – Ghost Tunnel

Ask the children to identify imperative verbs. What is their usual position in the sentence? How important is the order of the sentences? Which time connectives help provide a time sequence? ('First' and 'Then'.) **T14**

19 Hopewell Primary School – Year 3 Christmas Fayre

Compare this with the previous text. How helpful is the diagram? Is a written text clearer? Point out the use of devices such as arrows and bullet points.

Ask the children to write instructions for the route to a place known to them all. Encourage the use of both text and diagram and consider the merits of presentation using ICT. **T12, T13, T16**

20 How to stage a successful Christmas pantomime

Let the children discuss the text in pairs. What features are typical of instructions? Share findings, emphasising:

- Bullet points;
- Sequential order;
- Numbered lists;
- Imperative verbs;
- Headings;
- Clarity.

T14

How could the text be improved?

21 Jorvik

This is an instructional text about making a visit to the Jorvik Viking Centre in York. How good is the website presentation? Discuss the merits and limitations of this type of text. **T13**

Are the children familiar with timetables? Find other examples for comparison. Provide practice in using them. **T12**

Note-taking

22 Panto schedule

Investigate the text. Guide towards recognition of the note format. How is this obvious? (Words and phrases, not sentences; headings; organisational devices; abbreviations; symbols.)

Could the text be further abbreviated? Which words are the key words? Work together on identifying superfluous and essential words. (For example, 'hold' is expendable, but 'auditions' is essential.) **T17**

23 Flow chart of pantomime schedule

Remind the children of the content of the previous text. Discuss flow charts: their visual impact and ease of comprehension; a focus on key points. Investigate this text. Is it easy to follow? Is this layout more helpful?

Ask the children to create a flow chart, planning a future event (for example, an outing, a holiday or a sports tournament). **T17**

24 Week off school!

Who is the writer of these notes? (A schoolchild.) What about the intended audience? (The same child.) Ask the children to identify features of notes.

Make use of a recent announcement in your own school. Ask the children to write a summary in note form, with a friend as the intended audience. **T17**

25 Educational visit notes

Compare this with the previous text. Consider the probable writer, audience and purpose (a teacher's notes for a talk to parents). Which words distinguish the writer and audience from those of the previous text? (Language is more sophisticated; greater detail; clearer layout.)

Ask the children to identify ten or twelve key words or phrases. **T17**

Dictionaries and thesauri

26 Dictionary page

Make sure the chldren are familiar with the term 'definition'. Discuss the full function of a dictionary. Investigate the use of note forms (abbreviations; phrases; essential words; symbols; numbers; organisational devices; bold/italicised font). **T17**

Focus on the verbs defined. What are singular, plural and different person forms? **S10**

Select a section of words. Let the children work with a partner to find out:

- which ones they know;
- which ones they can spell.

Add them to their word collections and spelling logs accordingly. **W17, W19**

27 Thesaurus

Stress the clear layout. Familiarise the children with common terms and abbreviations. Compare the format with that of your school thesauri. Model write a text. Ask the children to use a thesaurus to replace some of the words. **W18**

Speaking and listening

Discuss the merits and limitations of the instructional texts in your classroom.

Try out oral improvements (for later writing).

Discuss when, why and how the children make notes.

TERM 3

Note-taking and letters

Range of texts including letters

28 Notes in class

What are these texts? (Notes.) Define the term 'note', differentiating it from 'letter'. Discuss the likely context, writers and intended readers (friends writing to each other during a lesson). Point out the casual style and layout. Ask the children to identify examples. **T20**

29 Claire

Compare this note with the previous texts. Do you think it's from a child or an adult? (Adult) What clues are there? (Mention of playground duty; better sentence construction; more sophisticated vocabulary and punctuation.)

Ask the children to write Claire's reply, using this note as a model. **T20**

30 Andrew

Debate whether this text is a letter or a note. Why is 'note' the better label? (No date or address.) Point out that this longer note comes close to being a letter. **T20**

Focus on the agreement of pronouns and verbs. Ask the children to write a note from Andrew to the Head, mentioning Claire, using pronouns where possible. **S1, S2**

31 Urgent!

What label would the children give this? Guide them to the term 'message' (or 'notice'). Investigate the layout, font, clarity and vocabulary. Point out that all these may be relevant to the message.

Provide the children with a current school or class subject to write a message about. Stress awareness of the audience. Encourage the children to use ICT to create a polished final version. **T20, T21**

32 Hopeless Hopewell!

Where is this text likely to be found? What features identify it as a newspaper report? (Layout; fonts; exaggerated language; paragraphs; details; quotes of interest from concerned parties.)

Revise note-taking. Ask the children to identify the key points in this report, and summarise it in note form for someone who has not read the article. **T25, T26**

Consider writing the events in a different form, for example in a story format. **T22**

33 Dear Mr Pickle

Ask the children to list the features which identify this text as a letter. Consider the formality of the layout, and the way the letter starts and ends. Investigate style and vocabulary, pointing out words which contribute to the threatening tone of this letter of complaint. **T16**

Focus on the use of commas to mark grammatical boundaries in sentences. Ask the children to identify instances; use these as models for other sentences. **S7**

34 Dear Jane

Compare this letter with the last one. Use the terms 'informal' and 'formal'. Ask the children to identify features that make this an informal letter (start; ending; punctuation, sentence-structure; vocabulary; tone).

35 Dear Mrs Wright

What type of letter is this? Is it formal or informal? Ask the child to identify the purpose of the letter (to answer, explain or appease). Consider the use of paragraphs, stressing how they help to communicate ideas clearly. **T16, T23**

Identify where commas are used to mark grammatical boundaries. **S7**

Let the children write an alternative letter from Mr Pickle, perhaps to a different reader, (for example, a child); or a letter beginning Dear Annabelle, written by Jane. Emphasise:

- correct layout;
- start and ending;
- division into simple paragraphs;
- the use of commas, when needed to mark grammatical boundaries.

Consider using ICT to produce and present the letter. **T23**

Link your work on letters to your study of a particular author. Let the children write letters to the author.

36 The Case of the School Meal Poisoner

What is the form of this text? Explain that a story form has been used here to recount an event. Use the previous texts dealing with this event to make notes on other points. Let the children use the notes to finish the story. **T22**

37 Health and safety

Discuss the factual nature of this text. Consider layout, sentence construction, paragraphs, and vocabulary. Why are some words in bold?

Identify words that the children do not understand. First provide practice in using different deciphering strategies. Then ask the children to use dictionaries to produce definitions. **S1**

Discuss ways to make notes on the content of a text. Stress the need to be aware of the reader of the notes. Will the notes be understood later? Ask the children to make notes on the first two paragraphs, identifying key points. **T25**

38 Health and safety – note-taking

Revise the children's previous work. How do these notes compare? Can you understand them? Discuss the content of the notes. Are key points covered? Consider the layout, font, and use of abbreviations. Who are the notes for? (Probably the writer, because of the abbreviations.)

Ask the children to use these notes as an example for writing a summary of Text 37. Set a word limit of about 100 words. **T26**

39 Dear Year 3

What is the purpose of this letter? (An invitation.) Investigate its style, vocabulary, and level of formality. **T20**

Brainstorm ideas for your own class invitation (inviting an Infant class to a storytelling session; a local author/illustrator/publisher to talk about the production of a book; a journalist to explain his style of note-making).

Write letters, perhaps in groups or pairs; improve the final published form using ICT. **T20, T21, T23**

40 Dear Stacey

Discuss the purpose of the letter. Emphasise its use of simple, clear paragraphs. Brainstorm ideas, and model write a further paragraph(s), inserted between the present paragraphs 2 and 3.

Ask the children to recount information about the play in the form of a newspaper article, perhaps as a review. (Refer to Text 32.) Encourage the children to use ICT to present their work. **T21, T22**

> ## Speaking and listening
>
> Hold a session in which the children use talk during the writing process, composing a letter to a friend, relative or teacher. Can they identify formal and informal language?

Alphabetical texts

41 Citizenship

Can the children identify this as an index? Discuss what an index is for and how it is arranged. Stress the use of alphabetical order. What common uses have the children found for using an index? (For example, locating items in a shopping catalogue.) Give the children practice in scanning the index, supplying you with a page number or a subject reference. **T17**

42 Glossary

The glossary is part of a book on citizenship. Explain that it links to the previous text. Discuss what a glossary is and investigate other examples. Using the previous text for support, ask the children to add to this glossary, perhaps using computers to help with layout. **T21, T24**

43–44 A–Z Lower Markham

Discuss the purpose of this index. Point out the use of abbreviations and the meaning of map references. Compare them with the index of an atlas. Stress the importance of font style and layout to the audience. **T21**

Focus on the detail of alphabetical order – the need to look beyond the first letter. Ask the children to put further abbreviations and road names (supplied by you) into the lists.

45 Website – BookBox

Which column has Anne Fine's name? Where is J K Rowling? Where would you put Nina Bawden? Remind the children of the skill of scanning. Discuss the layout, variations in font, and the benefits of alphabetical order, emphasising ease and speed of access to information. **T17**

Ask the children to add the names of other authors they have read.

46 Website – 24 Hour Museum Trail for Harry Potter Fans

Discuss the advantages and disadvantages of the layout. Could it be improved? How could use be made of alphabetical order?

Investigate commas, stressing their role in making grammatical boundaries. Question the children about the different uses made of commas. Ask the children to read the text aloud. Can they 'hear' the need for a comma? Try this exercise with a new text, where the commas have been removed or are in the wrong places. **S7**

47 Website – 24 Hour Museum Trail for Harry Potter Fans (continued)

Compare this with the previous text. How easy is it to use this list of museums? Can you scan the text for a place near you? Can you use it quickly and accurately? **T17**

Brainstorm ideas for improvements in presentation (varied fonts; headings; alphabetical order). Provide computer access for the children to produce a new, polished version. **T21**

48 Contents

Discuss where this text might be found. Give the children time to investigate the layout of the text. How is the text made more accessible to the reader? Point out the relevance of chapter headings; different fonts; organisational devices; clear layout; use of alphabetical order. **T17**

49 Index

Put the children in pairs. Provide practice in using the index. How quickly, easily and accurately can they find the answer? **T17**

Ask the children to find a resource book related to their current science topic (or sun/shadows). Let the children work in pairs, giving each other practice in making efficient use of the index.

Brainstorm ideas for a new book. Ask the children to prepare an alphabetically ordered index for the back of the book. Ask the children to consider the reader of the book. Will ICT improve the finished product? **T21, T24**

Use your current science topic, (or sun and shadows) as the basis for an alphabetically ordered glossary. Make sure the children think about the target audience, perhaps using ICT for their polished versions. **T21, T24**

50 Guide to Hopewell Primary School

Investigate the purpose and layout of this text. Is alphabetical order helpful? Consider other likely headings and sections for the rest of the guide.

Focus on the paragraph about the library. Talk about the Dewey system, and provide an opportunity for the children to gain experience in locating books, perhaps for current science, history or geography topics. Set fact-finding tasks, asking the children to be ready to explain how they locate their information. **T18**

Brainstorm ideas for a guide (for parents, new teachers or new pupils) to your school. Perhaps working in pairs, ask the children to decide on headings, put them into alphabetical order and to write the text. Provide computer access, so that the children can include ICT layout, font and organisational devices to bring their work to a polished form. **T21, T24**

Investigate the use of commas in the text, particularly those marking grammatical boundaries. **S7**

Speaking and listening

Share experiences from the children's fact-finding tasks. (Text 50)

Stress the need for clear explanations.

Hold a question and answer session: 'How would you find...?' Set questions which involve locating information from an index, or using the library to find a book. Answers could begin, 'This is what I did.'